A Hanna, Heastie, Tynes Family Story
(Second Edition)

By Judith Bell and Elva Heastie Jones-Gamble

Cover photo: Gram Ella Hanna

"A Hanna, Heastie, Tynes Family Story, Second Edition," by Judith Bell and Elva Heastie Jones-Gamble. ISBN: 978-1-63868-115-1.

Published 2023 by Virtualbookworm.com Publishing, P.O. Box 9949, College Station, TX 77842, US. ©2023, Judith Bell and Elva Heastie Jones-Gamble.

All rights reserved. No part of this publication may be reproduced, stored in a retrieval system, or transmitted in any form or by any means, electronic, mechanical, recording or otherwise, without the prior written permission of Judith Bell and Elva Heastie Jones-Gamble.

Acknowledgments

The formulation of the idea of this book began with many family gatherings at my grandmother's house in Miami, Florida years ago. It started with precious visits and casual conversations with beloved family members. Many family members deserve acknowledgements, but cannot all be listed here. First and foremost is gratitude to our Heavenly Father. It is from Him, all good things come. Secondly, a great part of this story would not have been possible if it were not for the knowledge, assistance, encouragement and stories recorded by my mother, Elva Heastie Jones-Gamble. Thanks also goes to our relatives, Iris Tynes, Danny Tynes, Ingrid Tynes Stuart, Idella Heastie Hogan, Ruby Hanna Ferguson, Helen Heastie Meade, and Nelly Hanna Major, who also contributed large parts of the story. Thanks to my brothers Brian and Carlton Jones who demonstrate the importance of staying connected to family.

As one reads this book of memories, one might find discrepancies in the facts within the various stories. I must include a disclaimer regarding any information that does not line up perfectly. Keep in mind that the purpose of this book is to record memories as each person sees them. Although memories might not hold true to all facts, memories are just as valuable and must be preserved, especially from ancestors who have passed on.

Stanford Hanna, one of the last family members still living on Pompey Bay, Acklins as of 2019

This book is dedicated to the memory of my grandmother, Katie Hanna Heastie and to the future generations of the Hanna, Heastie, Tynes family.

CROOKED ISLAND
The Bight
of Acklins
ACKLINS ISLAN
CASTLE ISLAND
Long Cay
Goat Cay
North Cay
Fish Cay
Guana Cay
Jamaica Cay
Snug Corner Sett.
Cotton Bay Cay

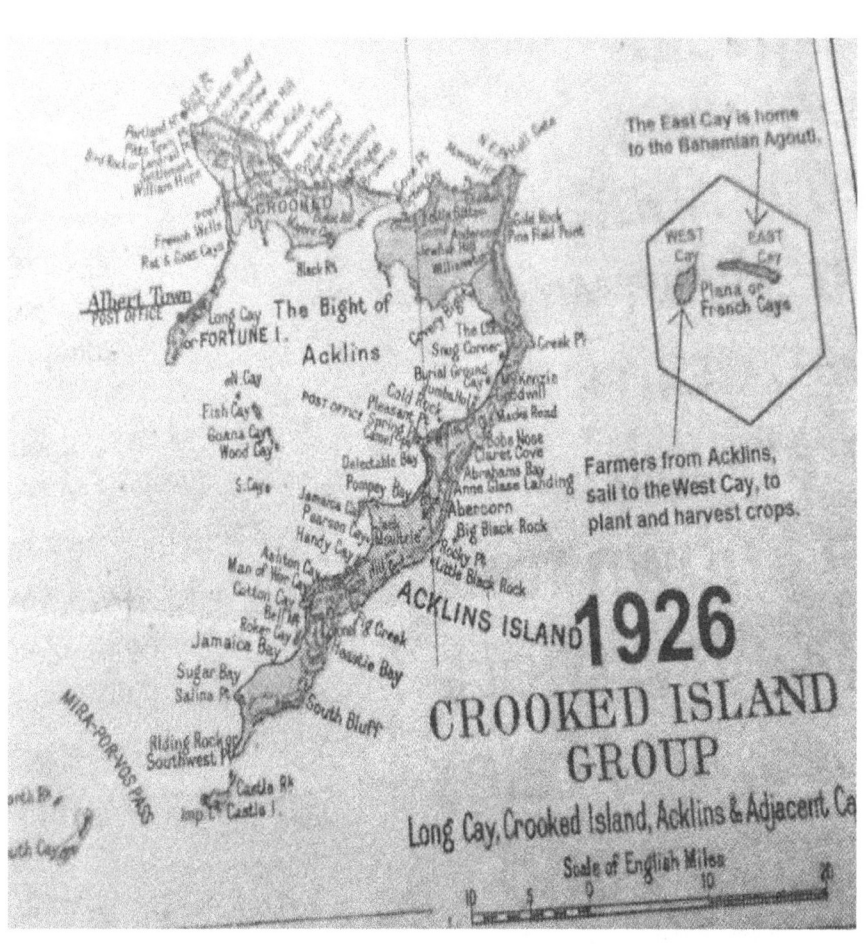

Maps of Acklins Island

Introduction by Judith Bell

Today if you were to visit Acklins Island, one of the lesser-known Bahamian Outer Islands, you would encounter beautiful undisturbed beaches, exotic animals, unusual plant life and rock formations. The warm clear waters are perfect for snorkeling and fishing. The island, just 92 miles long and 4 miles wide at the widest point, has just over 565 inhabitants according to the 2010 census. Public electricity was not available until 1998. It's an adventurer's paradise!

But who would have guessed that some settlements on Acklins Island were home to vibrant communities many years ago? Pompey Bay settlement was one of the original homesites for our family. This tight knit community was made up of descendants of slave owners and slaves brought over from Africa to work on the plantations. After slavery was abolished in the Bahamas in 1834, the descendants of Pompey Bay and Spring Point intermarried and became a proud and loving family. Our family, known by the surnames of Hanna, Heastie and or Tynes, endured through the atrocities of slavery and the bare necessities of island life, to go on to thrive and multiply. They passed down values such as faith and belief in God, a strong work ethic, positive self-esteem, endurance and a love for family. It is through knowing our heritage that we can teach our children to advance boldly into the future, carrying on the traditions of the family. Those traditional values are woven throughout the following stories of what life was like for our family, who lived there so many years ago.

The woman on the cover was Gam Ella Hanna. She was married to Thomas Napoleon Hanna, and lived in the Hanna Big Yard, the original Hanna settlement of Pompey Bay. Together they had 13 children, including Katie Hanna Heastie.

Family
A family is forever
It's the love in our hearts, our homes and our neighborhoods
It's brothers, sisters, mothers, fathers and
Every combination near and far
Everyone begins life as part of a family
Making the most of it is a lifelong opportunity
   - *Author Unknown*

Cover photo: Gram Ella Hanna, born 1845, died 1935

Beach scenes at Pompey Bay

A Brief History of the Hanna, Heastie, Tynes Family

Our family's origin begins with the settlement of three men in the Bahamas. These men were John Hanna and George Heastie, originally from Scotland, and Benjamin Tynes from England. After the colonies won the American Revolutionary War with Great Britain in 1776, some men who were loyal to Great Britain, fled from America. They were rewarded by the "Crown" with land in the Bahamas to settle and farm. These men were called "Loyalist" because they were loyal to Great Britain. Such was the case of some or all of the three men.

Slavery existed in the Bahamas at this time until it was abolished in 1834. The African heritage of the family began through the offspring of the black slaves and the white owners of the land. Unfortunately, the African roots of our family are much more difficult to determine, but the descendants took the surnames of the original Hanna, Heastie and Tynes. There was much intermarrying within the three families on the island and thus the family grew. Although the early family members were concentrated in the Pompey Bay settlement of Acklins Island, family members spread throughout the Bahamas, the Unites States and even the world. The following stories are a compilation of memories from a variety of family members who actually lived on Acklins Island, knew others who did, or family members who migrated from Acklins to Nassau and the US. There is limited editing so as to capture the original language of the story tellers.

Katie Hanna Heastie

Katie Hanna Heastie, 1890-1989

Katie Hanna Heastie was born and lived on Acklin's Island from 1890 until the early 1920s. She was a descendant of John Hanna (the Loyalist who first settled in Acklins). John Hanna's son was John Hanna II, whose son was George Hanna, whose son was Thomas Napoleon Hanna, who was Katies father. Katie married Edward Heastie, a descendant of George Heastie. Edward and Katie Heastie later moved to Miami, Florida, where she lived until her death at age 99, in 1989. She was proud of her Bahamian heritage and was a woman of immense self-respect and character. She had five children over 24 years of marriage and never considered marrying again, after the loss of her husband in 1934.

Many may wonder how Katie supported her family after becoming a widow during the Depression. She used the skills she learned from being a mother and excelled at washing and ironing clothes. This was during the days of scrubbing clothes by hand on the washboard and sometimes ironing without electricity. This was during the days when men wore long sleeve white shirts that were starched with starch made from Argo chunks and hot water. This was during the days of the six-day work week, without benefits. Her attitude made her a favorite of her six daily employers, whites in Miami, who could afford to hire help. They were especially kind to her. At the end of the day, she would come home exhausted after doing laundry by hand all day in the Miami heat. But she had great faith in God and He blessed her with good health, common sense and thrift.

She was particularly friendly, confident, and loved to square dance. Sometimes she would say, "Have you noticed, I have pretty legs!" She enjoyed crafts by hand and making fudge and cakes. Physically, she was about five feet tall, weighed 140 lb., had fair skin, keen features and long wavy black hair. Her focus for her children was to have high morals, a firm belief in God and to get an education.

Katie starting having fainting spells in her later years and would keep "smelling salts" to sniff when she felt a "spell" coming on. It was later determined she had a brain tumor. She said, "It will go with me to my grave. I will not have surgery at my age." We never knew if it was cancerous, but during her later years (1976-1989), it confined her physically, but not mentally. We assumed it was not cancerous because of the long number of years she lived after it was discovered. She remained cheerful and grateful, often dancing with her walker. Over ninety-nine-plus years, she outlived all her friends, yet St. Agnes Church in Miami, Fla. was filled at her funeral, because she was so loved by all.

The following notes were taken by her daughter, Elva Heastie Gamble: "I would ask her about her early life and make notes without her knowledge. These notes were taken over the years of Mom's confinement (1976-1989). We would spend evenings at the dining room table talking. Since she was advanced in age, I wanted to copy much of what she said for those not privileged to share these moments because of age or assignment at the time. I tried to save the flavor of her speech by copying the way she actually spoke, as we remember her. She had a strong island accent and I remember, as a child, trying to teach her how to pronounce words with the American sound. She would promptly correct me by saying, "It is the British who gave the English language to the Americans; how can you correct me?"

Katie Heastie with niece, Carrie and sisters Nellie and Vera

MY SISTERS AND BROTHERS

1. Castell Hanna	1873
2. Ida Hanna Tynes	1875
3. Dora Hanna	1877
4. Henrietta Hanna Ferguson	1879
5. Carrie Hanna Tynes	1881
6. Elvana Hanna	1882
7. Clarence Hanna	1884
8. Alfred Hanna	1886
9. William Hanna	1888
10. Katie Hanna Heastie	1890
11. Carmon Hanna Bain	1892
12. Richard Hanna (Died as a baby)	1894
13. Nellie Hanna	1895
14. Vera Hanna Dorsett	**1899**

"Memories of Life on Acklins Island"
by Katie Hanna Heastie

I was born in 1890 on Acklins Island, Bahamas, (Pompey Bay settlement), to Ella Hanna and Thomas Hanna, no (blood) relation. Ella's mother was Mary Collie who married Alexander Hanna. She was believed to be African. He lived on the other side of the island.

I went to school at Spring Point, another settlement east of Pompey Bay. My older brother, Castell, carried the family children from our settlement part way in his sail boat, to Camel Point. He would leave the sailboat anchored and we would walk the rest of the way to school. School was one room with ink wells in the desks. We sat on one long pew with desks in front. Those not old enough to use ink, used a slate and slate pencil.

When Castell was old enough to work on the farm, we were old enough to walk to school all the way. We had to cross five creeks. If the tide was high, we pulled our clothes up to keep from getting wet or a different father would take us across in a small boat with a staff. The creek from Delectable to Camel Point was the widest. The fifth creek was the deepest, but not over our heads. If rain caught us or our clothes got wet in the creek, we turned around and went back home. We went to school only three days a week, so we had to make up the lost day, the following day. Those who lived near the school, like Maude Moss and Raymon Heastie's grandparents, went to school every day.

Teacher with pupils at Cripple Hill School, Crooked Island. Circa February 1933.

((From Fairchild Botanic Garden))

An example of a one room school on Crooked Island

Sometimes when school was out, we would visit my grandmother, "Ma" (Mary Collie Hanna). She would always have something to give us, like bananas, grapes, green corn or a sweet potato she roasted. Our mother would fix a lunch pail to take to school. We left the pail at godmother Margaret Berry's house. We'd go there and eat before leaving for home. Most times there was no break. School was from 10 until 2:00. We did not get home until 5 or 6. We learned to read, write and figure. School went as far as standard 4. (grade 4)

Here is a song we sang as we marched into school:

Drive the nail aright boys!
Hit it on the head!
Strike with all your might boys,
While the iron is red!
Though you stumble off boys,
Never be down cast.
Try and try again boys,
You will succeed at last! (laughter)

As we got older, we learned to sew and make button holes. A cousin named Ma're Hanna taught me how to crochet at age 8. My sister, Dora, would take the older girls to dance right in the big yard. My daddy played the fiddle and so did his brother, William. The Constantina was played by my brother. When my older sisters had babies, midwives delivered the babies. "Ma" was a midwife and so were Kitty Ann Rolle and Della Bain.

Little before I got married, I started cooking. The stove was in the kitchen, which was a separate small building with a fire hut. There was a long iron on it. You set the iron pot on the iron rod to cook. We made fire from wood found about. We washed clothes in fresh water ponds after a rain. We made our own mattresses out of straw, and pillows from a bush with soft flowers that we dried. Once my father found a whole whale bone from its spinal column, washed clean and brought ashore from the tide. We used that for a favorite chair.

An example of a kitchen in a home on Acklins, circa 1900

The mail boat came about once a month to Spring Point. The Commissioner was there (Spring Point) and a prison. The Commissioner settled a case or it was sent to Nassau. The church and school were at Spring Point. People from Delectable lived a different, seemingly poorer life style. (thatched huts etc.) The houses at Pompey Bay were block with thatched roofs, later shingle roofs. Every family had their own hog pen. Sometimes the hogs were shipped to Nassau, live, for sale, in the family boats. They were given a memorandum to buy anything from the store you needed. Every family mostly had a boat.

I met Ed (Edward Heastie), your Papa, when he would come to visit on Sunday. His married sister, Silvie, lived in the Tynes yard. The Tynes yard was between the big yard and the church (St. Aiden's Anglican Church, Pompey Bay). The big yard was about 20 acres, walled in with rocks. We had cows in the pasture outside the big yard. The larger children milked the cows.

The men worked the farm and fished on Saturday. When they came home, in the evening, the wives met the boat and helped clean the fish. All fish not eaten that day or the next was corned (dried with salt). People never went without food.

St. Aidens Church, Acklins Island

I was confirmed in the church (St. Aiden's Anglican Church) at 13 years of age. The Hannas and Tynes were only two families living in Pompey Bay. The Tynes yard was separate from the Hannas. The Hannas and the Tynes built the church when I was a child. Uncle Ba-Kay (William Alexander Hanna) was the Catechist and he taught Sunday school. We learned the Ten Commandments from him. The Priest came from the Diocese in Long Cay for weddings and confirmations. His name was Father Duncan, an Englishman. To get to Long Cay, you would need to leave in the morning and get there by mid-day with fair wind on a sailboat.

My daddy, Tom Hanna, and his brothers went to trade school in Nassau. They learned to build boats and houses. There, they lived with Percy Hanna's mother, who was Lisa. Tom was a short man with straight black hair, swift in getting around, fair skin and blue eyes. The big house was built by George Hanna, my grandfather.

When my daddy, Tom, used to tell us about slavery, he said Queen Victoria did not send any white women when the slave ships brought the slaves and masters. (The masters had children with the slaves, which is why many family members were so fair.) The slaves were freed on the 1st day of August in 1840 and until today that day is a public holiday in the Bahamas.

Emma Daxon looked like a real African. She had very large bust, thick hair and a long bottom lip. She was a midwife and was real smart. She married a white man named George Heastie. Emma had a son named George Heastie. George married Martha Hanna, daughter of Stewart Hanna- no relation. I don't know where on Acklins they came from. Ma said that when the master landed, he gave the people his name. Every settlement had a master and they named the children after themselves. After freedom of the slaves, Queen Victoria sent ships to the Bahamas to take the slaves back to Africa. Uncle Ba-key's children married Emma Daxon's children (2 of them), Harriet and Ellen.

There was an African man who could not speak English at Spring Point. We passed his hut going to school. Aunt Essie and my bigger brothers used to poke fun at the man by saying, "Bushie Bushie" to the African and he would answer "Bushie Bushie" (laughter).

Slave records from George Heastie

All the men built their own boats (schooners). One would help the other. The head of every household usually had his own boat and some of the older boys in a family (also had one). The men also built their own houses. My father's (Tom) boat was named "Delightful". Charlie Tynes' boat was named the "Butterfly". Charlie was Francina's (Robinson) great grandfather. The Delightful was on a trip to Nassau and ran into a rock called "New Meter's Rock". Some call it "Hen and Chicks" because it was one large rock and several small ones. This was the first rock leaving Long Cay going to Nassau. The boat sunk. All were saved. I believe I was living in Inagua when this happened. Aunt Essie's brother had a boat named "The Sea Pearl".

I married Edward Washington Heastie October, 1911, in the church at Pompey Bay, by Father Franklin Deenza Brace. We stayed in Pompey Bay for about one week in my brother Clarence's house. Then we took a boat owned by Michael Cooper of Spring Point to Inagua, the 1st of November. The next day was All Saints Day. I lived in Inagua 5 years. Ed was running on a German steam ship that ran from New York to Jamaica. Ed only worked the part of the trip that went south from Inagua to Santa Mata and back to Inagua. The ship picked up laborers and freight and passengers, if any. I kept house, but Ed had a woman to do laundry for me. Inagua was like a city. Many people from Acklins lived there because of a chance to work on the ships. Ed had a good education and worked as a checker using figures.

On my first trip to Inagua, I took my niece, Carrie Tynes, to live with me. Carrie was about 5 years old. (Carrie's mother was Katie's older sister, Ida. Ida died and left many children. Different family members took her children to raise them.) My younger sister, Vera, came to visit me once or twice. We lived walking distance to Jib Bay, near St, Matthew's Church and next door to a commissary. We would walk about the distance of a block or two to Mr. Symonett at the dock who cleaned and sold fish from his boat. Inagua had a library, prison, and lamp post on the street. Levy Ferguson from Crooked Island used to ride his bicycle from one corner to the next and light the lamp post (kerosene lantern). Ed was saving money to take me on a trip to Jamaica on the ship he was working on, but the ship never came--- World War I started. Earlier, Ed had bought the material I made my wedding dress, from Jamaica.

I first knew Aunt Bird (Lena Heastie's mother) in Inagua. The ship brought her back from Jamaica where she lived with her husband. He got sick and died. At Inagua one got off the steam ship and transferred to a sail boat to go to Acklins. She had Lena with her as a little girl. The cost from Inagua to Long Cay was $1.00 and .50 for a child on the sailboat.

I got pregnant in Inagua 5 years later and went home to have my first baby (Idella Heastie Hogan). We never went back to Inagua, except to sell furniture and belongings. Ed's brother had a foundation of a house started in Spring Point on the Heastie yard. Ed finished the house – 2 rooms and he built a kitchen in the yard in the back. A couple of years later, I had another daughter (Viola Heastie Ho King).

On Acklins you ate fish and food from the sea, chicken, beef sometimes and wild hogs. We raised our own animals. (We got) milk from cows and churned our own butter. We raised sugar cane/syrup, corn, peanuts, peas, and lima beans. Meat was preserved with salt and drying. Kerosene lamps were used for light. I joined the Anglican Church at age 13 (confirmed) and became active in the church no matter where I traveled or lived.

A song we sang: (singing)

There is beauty all around when there's love at home.
There is joy at every hour when there's love at home.
Love at home, love at home,
There is joy every hour, when there is love at home.

My father was Thomas Hanna. He had 5 brothers—no sisters. His father was George Hanna. One of my dad's brothers, William, (aka) Ba-Kay, was 83 when he died. He had all of his teeth, but one. He was the Catechist in the church and taught me most of what I know about the bible. All of these brothers lived in the big yard of 20 acres, owned by their father, George Hanna.

George died when he was 86 years old. His tomb is there in the same big yard on Acklins. The brothers were Conrad (Aunt Essie's father who died when she was 3 years old), William (Ba-Kay), Walter (Lilla's mother's father), Peana, Thomas (my father) and Hugh.

All of the brothers went sponging and farming. They had cows and horses. They would ship them to Nassau to sell. To get them on the boat, they would walk them onto a plank over the water with rope around his neck. They could carry one horse at a time.
Some brothers went to Haiti to work. Hugh did not live to come back. My daddy was short in statue and very fair. Their mother was like a white woman---I think from Long Cay. All the boys were trained in a trade from Nassau. They all had a good education (for those days). All were carpenters. They made furniture as well as houses. The island had mahogany wood growing in the bushes and tall trees.

My daddy, Thomas, sponged, farmed and helped his boys build their homes. They built furniture too. Estelle took the bed that Conrad built from Acklins to Nassau and it was in her house every time I visited her.

When the brothers made a sale, sometimes they would buy rum and celebrate. My father was kind of quiet. My mother, Gram Ella, was the boss and disciplined us.

Many of the Cays did not have people living on them. (French Cay, Guana Cay, Nuss Cay etc.) When the men wanted to catch and corn fish, they would stay for days or a week there to corn the fish (salted and dried it). They would stay because it might rain and they would have to bring the fish in. Sometimes 2 or 3 of the men would sail to Haiti and sell the fish. They would buy coffee or liquor or anything else, and maybe sell that when they got back to Acklins.

My uncles never told us anything about slavery, only my grandmother. Her name was Mary Collie and she was married to Alexander Hanna. Mary was a slave, but she was not sent out in the field or farm to work. She did the cooking and kept house. She told this story:

"One day some slaves came in the house because it was raining. The master heard them talking and came in and asked what they were saying. The slaves quickly said, "More rain, more grass for master's horse." The master didn't believe them and gave them 50 lashes on their bare backs and sent them out to work."

By the time I was born, there were no masters... even my daddy never tell us about them. We always knew the white man knew more than us. We never tried to mix with them or take anything away from them. As a girl growing up on the island, the only white people there were like the Commissioner or school teacher and the priest. We never experienced any hatred. They were Englishmen. Even in Nassau later, when I was there, I never knew any hatred amongst the races. Nassau had quite a few white people. Harbour

Island people were mixed white and black (slaves). They mostly moved to Key West when they came to the U.S. They were called "Conkey Joe".

I never had a really bad storm (hurricane that she can remember) while I lived there. I heard they had a storm in 1866 and again in 1926. My daddy said that the night of the storm, they were building a schooner (sail boat). The wind blew the schooner from the beach to the house and the wind ceased. The house was not damaged. One of my daddy's boats was named "The Brothers". Castell (Katie's brother) built a boat and named it "Bright". Eugene named his "The Dew Drop". Willie Heastie had one named "The Whisper". Uncle Charlie Tynes had one named "The Butterfly". He had a nice wharf built with conch shells and rocks.

When the young men got engaged to marry, they started building their own houses. Most men would help them. By the time they got married, they moved in their house in the Big Yard. My brothers worked on the Panama Canal (the cutting of). Willie, Clarence and Alfred worked as laborers. When a friend or family member was coming home (from working away), they brought home mail or money. Sometimes they were paid with gold.

Uncle Clarence Hanna, (Katie's brother), his daughter, Linda and Walter Napoleon Tynes.

After I married on Acklins, my husband (Edward Heastie) went to America because work was plentiful. My second daughter, Viola (Heastie Ho King) was born on Acklins while he was in the away in the U.S.A. Kitty Ann delivered the baby. I believe Ed went to Charleston, South Carolina and there was an epidemic going on. He got the flu and almost died. He then went to South Miami, a place called "Peters", with other men from Acklins. I don't know the kind of work (he did), but it might have been harvesting the crop or clearing the land. He was tall and thin, but not very strong. (He was) a very caring man and tried to get the best care for his family. He was a strict disciplinarian about behavior in children.

Ed sent money by some people from Nassau Bay for our passage to Miami, Fla. The name of the ship from Nassau was the

"Yankton". The captain was George Smith, a black man married to Lareena Tynes, later Cowen after widowhood. We lived on 15th street N.W. in Miami. I never felt homesick because there were many people here from Acklins that I knew. I made one trip back home on the "Nassauvian". I got pregnant and had a stillborn female in Miami. After that, I went home when I was pregnant again. The child (male) lived 24 hours.

After the 1928 storm in Miami, many white people moved back north. Many small homes were for sale. Ed bought a 3 room, 2 porch house for $100.00 at George Pratt's suggestion, and moved us to Liberty City, (next door to George and Coolie Pratt). Aunt Coolie was Ed's niece. The 1928 hurricane caused a great flood from Lake Okeechobee. We had 11 relatives drown. Drowned were my sister Carmon and her 2 children, Arthur Tynes and 3 children, my sister Vera's husband and one child, Eunice Heastie and 1 son, George. Many friends from school and their families were lost. Many in-law relatives had heavy loss of life. Oh my!! (sadness)

Years later, my husband Ed was killed near Lake Okeechobee too. He was struck by lightning. After Ed's death, 3/28/1934, I tried to educate my children (so) that they wouldn't have to work as hard as I did to raise them. We were married 23 years, 5 months and 5 days. My father, Tom, died the same month as my husband. (Thomas Napoleon Hanna of Pompey Bay on Acklins)

In my years of work, after becoming a widow, I always had (a) job—never had to go to an employment office. One employer referred me to another… because I was one of the best ironers of white dress shirts and did such good laundry. I did laundry for white people.

Katie's five children (Idella, Viola, Elva, Grace and Carl)

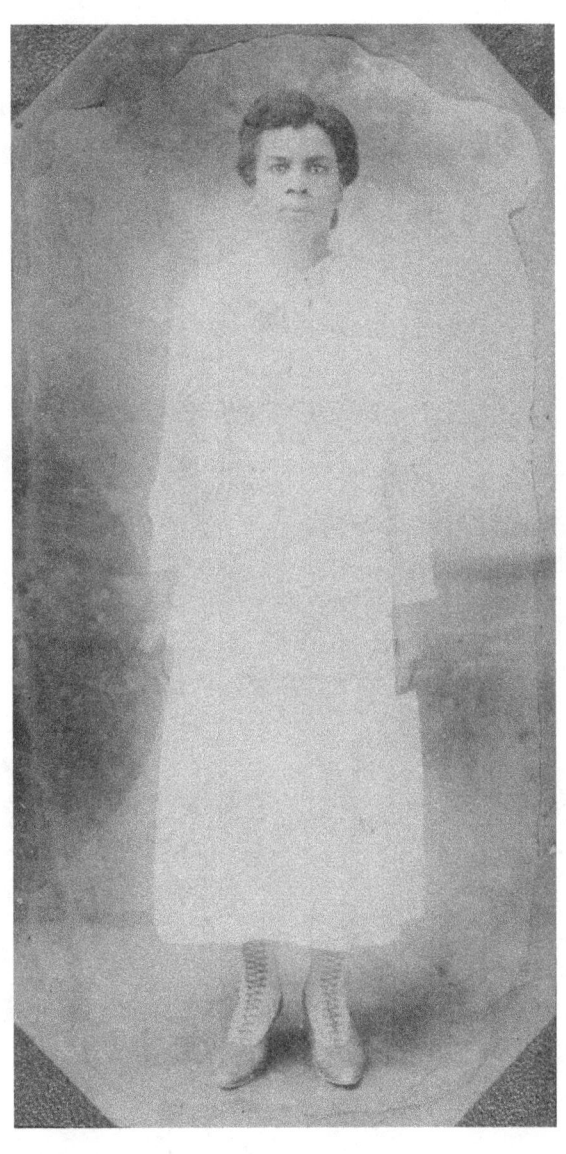

Carmon (Katie's Sister), who drowned on Lake Okeechobee 1928

Carmon's two children who drowned on Lake Okeechobee 1928

(Katies memories continue with life back on Acklins)

I was a child the day Aunt Julia Tynes (and 2 small sons) drowned. She was pregnant and lived in Pompey Bay. In the boat were Julia, Henry Tynes (her husband), her brother (Bruce Hanna), 2 young sons and an oldest son, Sammy Tynes. Julia could not swim. Julia and Henry were taking the children to school at Spring Point. The wind caused the boat to capsize. Julia was holding on to her son and her brother, Bruce, but she was going to drown them. The boys dove under water to free themselves from her. Her husband had left the boat halfway. (He had gotten off the boat earlier.)

The principal at the school heard the relatives moaning as they came to the school to tell him what happened. The principal let school out. The children at school walked to the site. She was wrapped in a blanket on the rocks, bleeding from her nose and mouth. Some of the people went down there where the boat was and pulled it on the shore of the bay. Only one boy was found. We believe a shark ate the other boy (one of the small boys). People took her to a relative's house at Spring Point. Then they carried the news to Pompey Bay. Some men who went to the bottom where the boat was and pulled it on shore, found a shark there. They believe it was the shark that ate one of the boys.

This was Ernest and Sammy Tynes' mother. She had many children. Aunt Julia was no kin to me, but she lived in the Tynes' yard and we children called her "aunt". She was a real stout, light skinned woman. I must have been about 10 or 12 when this happened.

We had a wake at her aunt's house that night in Spring Point. They carried her to the cemetery the next morning in a coffin Ned Hanna made, as he was the nearest carpenter there. The baby was in a small coffin and was buried on top of her in the same grave.
I can still see her on the rocks bleeding as this was the first person I had ever seen who drowned.

This was Ola and Baby's grandmother. Their father was Ernest. Julia had Edith, Sammy, Crissie, Wilmo, Copeland, Ernest and Dandy. Estelle, Clarence and I started to go back home, walking, but met our parents walking so we went back with them. That is how we got to attend the funeral. Oh my, how sad we all were!

Words to My Grandchildren by Katie

Work for a living in an honest way.
Remember the 10 commandments.
Thou shall not steal.
Honesty is the best policy. Thou shall not murder.
Be kind to your neighbors—love your neighbor as yourself. Be kind to all people.
Cast your bread on the water---will come back sevenfold.

Notes by Elva: Often during our talks, relatives would come by and visit Mama. Alphonso Tynes and Bertram Nimmo were two of Papa's nephews (his sister's sons). George, Arthur and Cyril Heastie were Papa's brother's (Uncle Willie) sons, who came to visit frequently also. Here were five handsome men who visited my widowed Mama often and brought great joy. They were generous toward her in money and farm goods. I loved the atmosphere when they were around. I was a grown, married woman before I realized they were Mama's in-laws, and not blood relatives. It made no difference. They had such great respect for Papa and affection for Mama. Now that Papa was gone, they faithfully visited her, recalling lively stories and experiences they each had with Papa. These were joyful times and I learned a lot about Papa listening to their recollections. One day during my time with Mama, Alphonso and Bertram came by and joined the conversation. Here are parts of the discussion:

Uncle Willie Heastie and son, Cyril

"A Conversation with Cousins Bertram Nimmo and Alphonse Tynes"
January 1984

Bert: Earliest memory? I spent most of my time in Inagua in the grocery business. I ran on a German ship as a checker. I was a glamour boy--smoked until WW1. Uncle Eugene owned the "Dew Drop" (sailboat). The Dew Drop broke up. Ed Heastie was on his way to Puerto Rico to visit Mary Ann, his mother's sister. The ship broke up (sunk) on the back side of Inagua.

Eddie Heastie, (Katie's husband) smoked a lot, but did not drink. He was the brains of the boys. Uncle Ed and I ran up to Belle Glade, Florida together. (This was after they moved from the islands to the U.S.). He had a car he made into a truck. One time he made a trip to Nassau on a sea plane (no airport) in the 1930s. We played dominoes a lot while on the "lake" (Belle Glade, Fla.). Uncle Willie (Heastie) built a little house on the lake for Ed. Ed stayed there and cooked for himself. (Migrants went up there to work the land.)

Alphonse came over to Florida from Acklins Island in the early 20s. He was a young man of 21 in 1928 when the great flood of Lake Okeechobee, Fla. flooded and drowned hundreds. He tells the story:

Several of us young Bahamian men went to Belle Glade, Florida, to clear the land by cutting cane for a white man, who was building a sugar mill. There were many snakes in the area. When we finished working, the white man told us to come back in two weeks to get paid. We lived in Miami and had hitched a ride to Belle Glade. In two weeks my friend and I came back and sat on a stump all day waiting for the white man to show up. He never did. It started to rain. We had an uncle living in one of the shacks near the lake in an area called "Chosen". We went to Uncle Ernest's shack to figure what to do next. (Aunt Julia, who drowned on Acklins, was Ernest's mother.) He was cooking a pot of beans and corn and invited us to eat. Darkness fell and the rain continued. Next door we could hear some young men laughing and playing cards. We decided to join them. As we stepped out into the darkness, the shack was swept away in a flood of water. We did not know that Lake Okeechobee was flooding. Darkness, logs and debris and were everywhere. My friend and I were holding hands trying to deal with the swift current and pitch blackness of night. He said, "Let go of my hand, I have cramps in my legs". I never saw him again. At that moment a bright light seemed to shine out of nowhere onto a nearby tree that had overturned. I swam with the tide and reached it. Somehow when day light came, I was still in that tree with snakes and other creatures. We lost 11 relatives who had come there as workers in that flood. Uncle Ernest was found alive several days later more than a mile away in some woods. My friend drowned.

(Today you can visit the area near Lake Okeechobee, Florida and see a plaque memorializing the many black migrant workers who were killed in the Hurricane of 1928. No names are listed.)

Hurricane victims to get funeral – 70 years later

Associated Press

The caravan of trucks passed through the West Palm Beach neighborhood, carrying a load of dead bodies as if it were wood.

It was an unceremonious procession to an unmarked grave for 674 black farm workers who were killed — mostly drowned — when a hurricane destroyed Lake Okeechobee's dikes, flooding Everglades communities in 1928.

At least 1,836 people were killed by the storm, one of the deadliest of the century. While many white residents got proper burials, the black farm workers were buried next to the city's dump.

The bodies were dumped into a deep ditch, covered over with dirt and forgotten.

Until now. A funeral is planned for Saturday in their memory. Participants will walk four blocks to the burial site — marked now only by boulders and wooden stakes. There, a memorial service will be held.

"This will be the funeral procession that these folks didn't have," said Robert Hazard, organizer of the event and chairman of the Storm of '28 Memorial Park Steering Committee.

However, the long-overdue tribute is in peril of further delay as another deadly hurricane makes its way across the Atlantic. Forecasters say Hurricane Georges, which battered the islands of the Caribbean this week, could be pounding across South Florida by week's end.

Hazard said his committee has sought help from the city and other organizations to place a marker on the site where the farm workers were buried.

Lonnie Colbert, 92, remembers seeing the trucks drive through his neighborhood on their way to the ditch. He said police told residents to stay indoors and not look at the trucks as they passed.

"The bodies were loaded in there like you would load wood, and a tarpaulin covered them," Colbert recalled.

Hazard said he's been told by city officials that the city cannot build a memorial on the land because it is privately owned. The committee doesn't have the funds to buy the land, he said.

"It's a disgrace that it's left unattended, abandoned and forgotten by the people of Palm Beach County for 70 years," he said.

26

Idella Heastie Hogan 1915-1998 by Elva Gamble

Idella, affectionately called Dell, was the first of Mama and Papa's (Katie and Edward) children, born in 1915. I believe she was the favorite of all her siblings. Dell was compassionate, loving, generous and kind. When our father was killed suddenly, by lightening, she immediately stepped in his shoes and became the visionary for the whole family. We jokingly called her "our daddy" when she seemed to be too controlling. Dell became a registered nurse and married James Hogan, her teenage sweetheart. James later became a medical doctor. They had no children, but together, we loved them dearly. After the death of our mother, Katie, she asked me "I wonder if Mama knew how much I loved her"?

That is a question I (Elva) wonder today--did Dell know how much her siblings loved her? I encouraged Dell to write down some of her memories during her last years.

"I Remember"
by Idella Heastie Hogan

The first house I remember living in (on Acklins Island) was down the road from the one I was born in. It was a white, two room framed house, sparsely furnished. One of my earliest memories was one night, my mom (Katie Hanna Heastie) was trying to get me to go to sleep. When I refused, she laid down on the side of the bed with me. I grabbed the hem of her skirt, hoping when she got up, I would awaken, as she yanked her skirt. It never happened.

There was no glass or screens on the windows or doors. The windows swung out like the doors. If the doors and windows were closed at the same time, the house was very dark. The roof was made of tin, and I love hearing the rain drops falling on it. Even to this day, I like listening to the rain drops falling on my windows and roof.

An example of an early house on Acklins

The kitchen was built separate from the house in the back with a thatch roof, and a hard dirt floor. There was some type of a grill we used for cooking and tree branches or twigs for fuel. We often gathered the twigs from the woods that surrounded our house on three sides. The front of the house was on the beach. When the tide was out, I could walk into the ocean the length of three city blocks and it was no deeper than a 4-year-olds knees. Further out and to the east of our house, there was a royal blue area with white foam; we called "the blue hole". The natives said that the reason that area was darker than the rest of the ocean, was because that was a bottomless part of the ocean. The fisherman liked to go there because fish were plentiful. Many lost their lives by getting too close. (If one were to try to locate this area today, this provides lots of clues as to where the location was, since the tide and deep blue area of the ocean would still be there today.)

On the first Christmas, that I can remember, my sister (Viola Heastie Higgs Ho King) and I hung a sock on a nail and Santa brought each of us a biscuit that was sweet. We were so happy. We never had toys. We never knew what toys were. Children played games that our parents played when they were children. Almost every evening, they would tell us about our roots. That was interesting. I still talk about those stories. I wish I could hear them now.

This house I lived in was on an island in the Bahamas, called Acklins. The settlement was Gold Rock. The only mode of transportation was your feet. There was one road. One evening, my father closed all the windows and doors because a hurricane was coming. The waves would crash against our house with spray, hitting the tin roof. My parents seemed concerned, but I felt safe because we were together. God protected us and kept us safe. The last thing I heard my father say to my mother was that the barometer was falling. I drifted off to a peaceful sleep, wondering where the barometer was or where it was falling from. Oh well, I'll look for it in the morning. I never did.

Later we migrated to Miami, Florida because it was said that work was plentiful. Many other relatives from the islands migrated also. My mom had three more children in Miami.

I remember when my sister, Elva, was born. I was told to sit on the porch when Elva was born. The midwife came and later told me I had a sister. I never remembered my mom being pregnant. I had begged my mom for a baby, and then Elva was born. I was crazy about her and called her "my baby". But I got tired by the time Carl (Katie's 5th child) was born. I had to carry all three children (Elva, Grace and Carl) around wherever I went. That was my mom's way of keeping me out of trouble. Grace was born on a Sunday. I named her Grace because of the rhyme, "Sunday's child is full of grace". Elva said she remembers being told to sit on the porch when our brother Carl was born too, in Liberty City. There were no cars to come down our street in Miami. Only one man had a truck on our street. I remember playing ball when Carl was born in 1930.

Elva, Grace and Carl with cousins in Overtown, Miami

I remember Pappa. Papa, (Edward Heastie), was a tall, thin, handsome man with dark piercing eyes. His moustache covered his upper lip which tickled my cheeks when he kissed me. He was 45 years old when I was born and 64 when he died. I always thought he was an old man mainly because of his physical actions. When getting out of a chair or just walking, it seemed as if all his joints were stiff. But he was not considered disabled. Being unskilled, he made a living doing odd jobs and migrant farm work.

He was quite a disciplinarian. When he gave you an order to do something, he meant for you to do it then. If he had to tell you a second time, it was followed by a blow with something near his hands. Today one would call it abuse. But then it was called discipline. However, there was lots of love. He played games with my four siblings and me, and was always ready to tell us stories. He was not a church going man, but he saw to it that every Sunday, we were in somebody's Sunday school or church.

He prepared breakfast for us every morning, except Sunday. That was his day of rest. Mom cooked that day. On Sunday, my parents would read the bible together and sing hymns as if they were in church. We lived on Acklins Island until the early 1920's, and then moved to Miami, Fla. My father died in Florida. Though he has been dead for over 69 years, I wish he could have lived longer to see how well his children turned out. Almost daily I see or hear things that make me remember Papa, such as watching my gardener do my yard, reading about Lake Okeechobee, or looking at the vegetable farms.

My father did not get married to my mother, Katie Hanna, until his parents died. He was a devoted, loving family man. He loved to discuss religion and play checkers. When he would get home from work, he would eat and sit on the front porch until night. It was hot in Miami and there was no air conditioning in those days. He smoked a pipe and would tell us stories. But most of the time, he was a quiet man, like my brother Carl, and had short patience like my sister Grace. When we were older, we had to clean the house spotless before we could go somewhere. Mom would direct us to ask permission from our dad. He was very strict. But I remember him washing our feet at night after playing all day. We knew he loved and cared for us.

In 1934, he turned 64 on March 2, but died later that month on March 28. My mom was 44 when he died. She had 5 children and the youngest were Elva, age 8, Grace, age 6 and Carl, age 4. My dad was working on a farm in Belle Glade, Florida on Lake Okeechobee. There were lots of settlements around the lake where the migrant workers stayed. He might be gone for months working there before coming home. A telegram came and said he had died. When he died, the undertaker brought me to identify his body since I was the oldest child. He had a big blister on his chest, his jeans were split and his shoe had a burned spot. There was a storm and he had gone under a tree to stay dry. Lightning struck and killed him. My younger sisters and brother had just come home from school. My mother was at work. She worked, but not regularly. The minister who did the funeral was a friend of his and belonged to a Holiness Church, which is where the funeral was held. It was a very sad time for us all. My mom didn't know how she would care for us after my dad died.

Note added by Judith Bell:

Edward Heastie was buried in the "colored" cemetery in Miami Florida. It was called Solomon Cemetery after Sam B. Solomon, founder of Solomon's Funeral Home in 1922. Today it's called Evergreen Cemetery in the Brownsville subdivision of Miami. This is located near another historic colored cemetery called The Pharr Cemetery, which was for the more affluent blacks.

"Papa" Edward Heastie

Flora Clark Heastie, Edward Heastie's mother

Viola Heastie

Elva Heastie

Grace Heastie

Carl Heastie

Cousin Iris Tynes

Granddaughter of Ida Hanna and daughter of Hilton Tynes

Cousin Iris Tynes
by Elva Gamble

Family support was an important value we shared. One example is the time my cousin, Iris Tynes came to the U.S, from Acklins to help me at the request of my mother. In the spring of 1957, I (Elva) set out with my husband and two small children to live in Michigan, about 1500 miles from my home in Miami, Florida. This was a difficult time for my Ma (Katie) who never wanted us to live far away, but by now had become used to saying good-bye to me. She decided I needed some help with my small children. We had no family in Michigan, so she asked her younger sister, Nellie, living in the Bahamas, to come along with me for a year. Nellie declined due to age or the climate in Michigan, but asked Iris, a cousin to come instead. Iris was 21 years old as I recall, beautiful, energetic, gentle, teachable, and oh so willing to please. She gave every evidence that she was happy to see these areas of America that otherwise might have escaped her. I tried my best to help her adjust and enjoy her time with us. She was a gift from God, and to this day, I give thanks for her and my mom for the suggestion. This should give you a glimpse of how family supported each other in our time. Here are memories of life on Acklins Island by Iris Tynes during the time she lived there from 1930-1950:

"Memories of Life on Acklins Island from 1930-1950"
by Iris Tynes

I was born and lived in Acklins Island from 1930 to when I moved to Nassau in 1950. I remember many things. One of Aunt Katie's (Katie Heastie) favorite sayings was: "He who steals my purse, he steals trash, but he who steals my good name, steals all that I ever possessed." I am not sure, but I believe the English writer, Shakespeare, said those words. Bahamians loved the Queen of England, especially Queen Victoria. At that time the Bahamas were colonized by the British.

Pompey Bay was the settlement on Acklins where the families lived. Eleanor and George Hanna were the owners of the Big Yard at Pompey Bay, and called it "Speedwell". Pompey Bay got its name after a slave named "Pompey". Eleanor and George's sons, Conrad Crosby, William Alexander, Thomas Napoleon, Henry, Walter and Hugh lived there along with many other family members. The area was about 20 acres enclosed by a rock wall with two gates in the front and back and called The Big Yard. The beach was about 300 feet from this enclosure. A concrete dock was built seaside. Cows, sheep, goats, chickens and pigs were kept in the pasture right outside the walls. The houses were built with crack rocks, lime and sand. The roofing was made with wood, boar and shingles. The church separated the Hanna's Big Yard from the Tynes yard. The Heasties lived mainly in Spring Point on Acklins Island.

The family church was St. Aidens Anglican church. The first bishop was Bishop Shedden, an Englishman. In those days all bishops were English. St. Aidens is still standing on the original site between the Hannas Big Yard and the Tynes estate., although in disrepair. The building was designed by a visiting priest, a friend of Bishop Shedden. The first catechist was the son of George

Hanna and Eleanor Heastie Hanna. His name was William Alexander Hanna, born in 1843 and died in 1921. His tomb is in the church yard. Other catachist to follow were Matthias Tynes and Napoleon Tynes. The church was the center of life there.

St. Aiden's Anglican Church at Pompey Bay , circa 2018

Altar at St. Aiden's in Pompey Bay, Acklins, 2018

Christmas was a special time of year. To let us know that Xmas was near, about two weeks before Xmas, the young boys would go from house to house singing and beating drums and asking for other boys to come out to join the fun around a bond fire. We prepared for Christmas by painting the houses. It was called "white washing". All the houses were white, made from stones and lime that was made by the men for building. It was similar to cement. Some of the houses that were built during slavery can still be seen there today. Slavery was abolished in the Bahamas and the Caribbean in 1834 and in 1838 all slaves were set free. After preparing the house with new curtains and a special bedspread, we dressed our Xmas tree. The Xmas tree was a special tree that grew wild in the bushes, but bloomed with beautiful flowers similar to orchids and had the most beautiful fragrance. The day before Xmas eve, cows, pigs, goats and sheep would be slaughtered for the Xmas day feast. Fish, crawfish and conch were the chief seafood. Crab and rice, pigeon peas and rice, beans and rice would be cooked. Cakes included pound cakes, coconut cakes, coconut tarts, Benny cakes, flour cakes and peanut cakes. Potato bread made with coconut, corn bread, and flour bread (white) were prepared for Xmas day and after. On Xmas eve there would be a mid-night service at St. Aidian's Church. After our service was over, we traveled to a nearby settlement called Morant Bay where there were two churches, a Baptist and a God of Prophecy we called "The Jumper church", because they jumped and shouted. After their midnight service, they had "Rushing" where we "rush" until daylight, to the music of drums, organs, guitar and accordion. This was like a Junkanoo. On Christmas night a concert was held where young and old, took part in the play, "The Nativity". We sang Xmas carols, read poetry, sang solos and performed short skits. There was always dancing. New Year's Eve church service at midnight was called "Parting of the Old Year'. After 12 midnight, everyone shared in the New Year's greeting and wishes. This chorus was sung for the New Year. "Happy New Year, Happy New Year, You happy, We happy, Happy New Year!" It was a happy time for all!

Uncle Ernest Heastie and relatives

Children were to speak when they were spoken to and answer to a call. They were to be seen and not heard. Children sat by themselves when visitors came around. You had to peep through the hole to see who was visiting. If you wanted to play or visit your friends, permission would have to be granted. If not, you were beaten with a tamarind switch. Everybody's child was like your own. On Sundays, children went to church three times, for Sunday school, church service and Evensong. If you were rude, your teacher would beat you and if you told your parents, you would get another beating. The children then, unlike the children of today, had little to eat. Bread and tea were for breakfast or corn meal porridge. For lunch at school there was bread and marmalade with lime aid or water or bread and sweet milk. For supper there might be peas and grits, fish, conch, crawfish, peas and rice, pea soup and dumplings or bean soup and dumplings. Grits were eaten with **soup** also. There was a special meal on Sundays. Sodas were cooled in the well or buried in the cool sand near the water on the beach. There were no fat children or fat adults. Unlike today, we were very healthy except for a cold and cough sometimes. We rarely saw a doctor and only on occasions if the bush medicine did not cure the patient.

We attended the Pompey Bay All Age school, built in 1903. It was 50x25 feet and all the children were taught in one room. The school was located about 2 miles from the Big Yard, near the beach. The original school was destroyed by a hurricane and the present school was built further inland. The education system was based on the British system because the Bahamas were a British colony. The textbook was the "Royal Reader". School rules were strict and had to be obeyed. You had to have your hair combed and brushed, teeth cleaned, fingernails cleaned and clothes cleaned and ironed. School hours were from 9:00-3:00, except on Fridays, 9:00-12:00. Morning assembly was held by the entire school every morning. We had prayer, sang a song, inspection of nails and clothes and exercise. After which we returned to the classroom singing our time tables from 2 to 12 every morning. Xmas holiday was 2 weeks, Easter was 1 week and summer was 6 weeks. There was one head master, one assistant teacher and monitors. Children entered school from grade 1 to 3 and then 3 to 6. If you failed to be tidy, you would be sent home. You would be whipped for being late or for not doing your homework. Before the school was built, parents hired private teachers for their children. One teacher was James Sands.

We traveled by sail boats that the men built. Some men were boat builders for their occupation. Some other jobs men had were building contractors, carpenters, farmers, spongers, masons, tailors and fishermen. George Hanna was a shipwright and built 3 schooners. Conrad Hanna and his brothers built the "Ursula Bright" and "Delightful", names they gave their boats. It used to take about 15 days to reach Nassau when the wind was calm, on a sail boat. When the wind was favorable, it was about 8 days. Everyone traveled by sail boat to all the islands. Some would be so sea sick.

When someone died, we had a "wake". A wake was always kept for the dead body because in those days the body was only kept for about 24 hours before burial. So, we would sit up all night singing until morning. During the night, coffee, tea, sweet milk and Johnny Cake were served. Nobody wanted to look at the dead face because death was a frightening experience on the island. Three and four families slept together for days during the burial time.

Modern day grave marker at Pompey Bay

Old tomb at Pompey Bay

Dating was different back then. To woo a young lady, you needed the permission of the father. You were allowed three visits to the house before your intentions were asked for. Afterwards your visits would cease if your intentions did not meet the parent's approval. Your visit to the house was no later than 9 o clock. After 9:00, a hint was thrown at you to leave. (ie. a cough or clearing of the throat) Weddings were held on Wednesdays. Before the wedding, the bride was confined to her chambers or room before she goes out. Two days prior to the wedding, the groom had no access to the bride, and if he had a message for her, he would send it. Weddings usually took place in the mornings and the celebrations went on all day and night. The reception house was enlarged by removing the partitions so that there would be enough space for the bridal party and guests. A large wedding bridal party will have about seven bride's maids, one of which would be the maid or matron of honor. This wedding will be called "Rainbow Wedding" because the bridesmaid's dresses would be in pastel shades like the colors of the rainbow. The bride would be in a white gown, veil and train.

For the reception a cow, pig, goat or sheep was slaughtered and cooked for the occasion. There was also peas and rice and lots of cakes (pound cake, coconut cake, flour cakes) and a special bridal cake). The music was provided by a guitar, goat skin drums, and accordions and a saw raked with a dull knife. The bride and groom would dance the first number, followed by the bride's maids and grooms 'men. Then the other guests would dance the night away. The bride and groom would dance a beautiful waltz. The groom wore scissor tail coat, derby hat and a walking cane. The bridal party walked to the church for the ceremony. There were no cars in those days. But there was lots of excitement and enjoyment! Oh, happy days!!!

The men would help each other build a house right in the Big Yard for the newly married couple. We may have been short on material things, but we were rich because we had the love and support of our family members. We knew who were and that there was unconditional acceptance.

Iris Tynes

Hilton Tynes, Iris Tynes father

Cousin Ingrid Tynes Stuart

Ingrid Tynes Stuart was born in Nassau, Bahamas to Denzil Wardell Tynes of Pompey Bay, Acklins and Ethel Tynes (nee Neely) of Mangrove Cay, Andros Island. Denzil Tynes is the eldest child of Hilton and Bertha (Hanna) Tynes both born at Pompey Bay, Acklins Island. She is the great-granddaughter of James Tynes and Ida (Hanna) Tynes. A true Hanna, Heastie, Tynes descendant, Ingrid is proud to boast her lineage to our original fore fathers as a 7th Generation offspring of John Hanna, 6th Generation offspring of George Heastie and 7th Generation of Dr. Benjamin Tynes. She presently lives in Pembroke Pines, Florida with her two sons, Lenville Tynes Stuart and Akeem Tynes Stuart and husband, Leonard Stuart. Her siblings and immediate family members include: brothers, Denzil Wardell (deceased),and Ian Tynes of Nassau. Aunts: Iris Tynes, Eltha (Dancie) Tynes Knowles, Nassau, Velma Tynes Richardson, Philadelphia, uncle, Hilton Kendal Tynes, Florida.

"For Ole Times Sake"
by Ingrid Tynes

Whenever I feel nostalgic, my mind automatically focuses on our family and the wonderful experiences I had of sharing, visiting, caring and loving each other when I was growing up in Nassau. Bahamas.

The weekends in our family homestead were spent visiting other family members or with them visiting our family. Saturdays were spent in the yard with my grandfather, Hilton, and his brother, Walter and other first cousins. I remember it would always be 5 or 6 older men gathering, sitting on the back steps or just in the backyard or porch talking and sharing a few drinks. They spoke of the family and of Acklins and shared old-time jokes. They were always so happy to be in each other's company. The men included Clarence "Chippy" Tynes, Harold Bowe, Harlington Hanna, Luther Munroe, Roland Tynes, Ted Tynes and Errol Hanna.

The family members visited at any time. There was always an open door at my grandparent's home. The family that lived in the same neighborhood like Donald & Louise Tynes and children, Lawrence & Barbara Tynes and children, Emmet Tynes, Cleo Tynes and family, E.R. Hanna & Carol and family, Wilton Hanna & family, never passed the house without stopping in for a minute or just tooting their car horns to say hello. Kendrick Hanna, Ivan Hanna, Lydia "Glen" Lightbourn were regulars and Oscar Hanna lived with the family.

And then there were the visits by family from the United States, like Carrie Tynes and Ethel Tynes, who were my grandfather's sisters and Katie Hanna Heastie, who was my grandfather's aunt. His nieces were always so excited on their visits like Francina Robinson and Eleanor Miller who gave us the United States experiences. Ruby Ferguson & family always stopped by every trip to Nassau. Then came the nephews like Eugene and Walter

Lewis. But not only did we experience our family on the Tynes side, but we also had my grandmother's side, the Hannas, such as her brother, Crosby Hanna and nephew Lofton Samuel Hanna and his wife, Ruth and so many others. These were very, very happy visits. When our family came from Acklins island, like my great grand aunt, Nellie Hanna, who lived with family for a while, we knew what Acklins was like, without even visiting.

I know that Acklins is a beautiful island that must be quiet, green and of solid, rocky land. I know the water is clear and blue. I know about the sisal, the horses, the outside kitchen, the beautiful Anglican Church, Pompey Bay School, the large mosquitoes and lots of fish and conch. I have never even visited Acklins, but I know that Acklins is my home too.

I observed, at a young age, how the family treated each other. How there were so many warm greetings, the serving of Bahamian foods and the exchanging of gifts. No one came or left empty handed. There was always something to share or exchange, be it limes, avocado pears, sour-sop fruit or guavas from the yard or flour cakes, coconut cake, Benny cake or potato bread.

I learned our family history from listening to my grandmother, Bertha Tynes and other family members. My grandmother was one of the family historians and many came to hear the history. I knew the characteristics of our family. I knew the connection of everyone that visited. I saw them at weddings, funerals and just around town. I learned exactly who I am, where my emotions, facial features, talents, and strengths and weaknesses came from. Today, with pride, I am eager to identify who I am, a member of the Hanna, Heastie, Tynes family!

Denzil Tynes

Ethel Tynes

Vera Hanna Dorsett

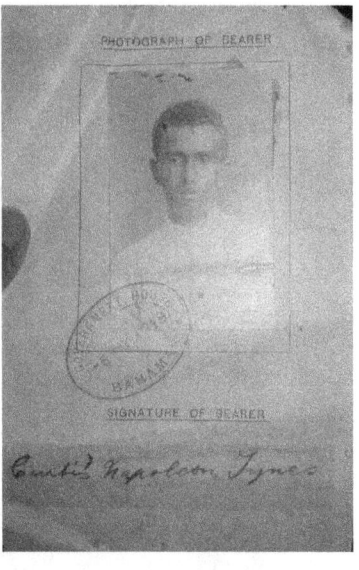
Curtis Napoleon Tynes

Cousin Danny Tynes

Danny Tynes is a cousin who lives in Nassau and who was very active in the Hanna, Heastie Tynes reunions which began in the early 1980s. He is a descendant of Dr. Benjamin Tynes, whose son was Dr. William James Tynes, whose son was Charles Tynes, whose son was Alvin Tynes, whose son was Clarence Tynes, who was Dannys father. Danny and his wife, Cynthia have been gracious hosts to family members who came from near and far. The following story is one he wrote about his memory of traveling to Acklins as a child.

"A Child's Trip to Acklins Island, Bahamas"
by Danny Tynes

Fore day that summer morning in 1949, my sister Sharon and I were awakened from dreamland by Mummy. We struggled to stand up in the middle of the bed and instinctively rubbed our eyes to adjust to the overhead light in the room. We were not pleased to have our sleep disturbed so early in the morning.

In the midst of warm bath and clean clothes, Mummy declared Daddy was taking us to visit our grandparents in Acklins (from where we lived in Nassau). Our younger brother, Maurice, was still in diapers and not permitted on this trip.

Daddy's friends called him "Chippie" because they said he resembled a popular local merchant whose last name was Chipman. By Bahamian standards, Chippie was a big man. He stood six feet one inch and weighed more than two hundred pounds. Chippie wore a smile that matched this bulky physique.

Chippie, a show-off that he was, wanted everyone to know he was taking the older of his three children to meet his "Papa" and "Mama". His huge oval face lit up like a Christmas tree! MAN, he was anxious to show off his children to his Pompey Bay, Acklins relatives. Chippie wore that BIG SMILE from home, to the mail boat, to Acklins.

The Mail Boat

The MV Air Pheasant was an entirely new experience for Sharon and me. For all we knew, it was an ocean liner! We were relieved to find our frisky cousins Leonard and Junior Tynes, Uncle Bruce's younger sons, running up and down the deck of the sailboat and climbing the bow railings to look down at the sea. To prove I wasn't afraid, I too pulled myself up on the railings to glimpse at the small waves below, heaving bits of rubbish between the boat's waterline and the dock. Sharon refused to have a look. Close by in a conversational circle were Chippie, Uncle Bruce, and three or four other men, standing and chatting with occasional outbursts of laughter.

The Air Pheasant held a government contract to deliver mail to the southern Bahama Islands. She supplemented this lean income by subsequently transporting freight and passengers. This morning the Air Pheasant pushed off from the City Lumber Yard Dock and steamed toward Long Cay. On the way, the Air Pheasant made scheduled stops to Rum Cay, Clarence Town, and Crooked Island before disembarking us at Long Cay. Afterwards, she took provisions for the lighthouse keeper, stationed at Castle Island, which is a cay off the western shore of Salina Point, Acklins. From there the Air Pheasant set sail for Inagua, her last leg of the voyage.

Our first night at sea didn't go as planned. At bedtime, daddy led us to our cabin. The interior of the vessel reeked with the smell of diesel oil. As a result, the Captain Anthon Lockhart, offered Daddy his cabin on the bridge. This became our bedroom for the remainder of the voyage.

Long Cay

Daddy got us out of bed, dressed and on deck in no time to wait our turn to disembark at Long Cay. We joined a band of noisy passengers with bundles of personal possessions, who jostled turns to be lowered to the dinghy that would ferry us to shore. A brilliant overhead light lit the port side of the mail boat, dispelling the immediate darkness. Some strong arm lifted the children over the side of the mail boat to a crewman, dangling on a rope ladder by hand and foot, half-way down the side the side of the boat. A second crewman standing in the dinghy, bobbing in the black waves, caught each child and pacifically placed us in the dinghy. The elderly and women were assisted into the dinghy, while the hardy made their own way down the ladder. Personal possessions followed.

It would be an amazing sight, to a supposed bystander, to see this jumble of humanity and freight, huddled together in a twelve-foot, homemade wooden hull boat, making its way from the mail boat in Crooked Island Passage to Long Cay. When the dinghy was full, the man who caught the children, ambled his way to the stern, took up the oversized oar, put its broad end against the boat and with all his might, shoved the dinghy off from the mail boat, sculling toward a distant glimmering light. On reaching the shore, it turned out this light was given off by a hurricane lantern, hoisted on a pole as a signal to passing ocean-going ships, of impending danger of nearby reefs, lining Albert's Town shore.

The Air Pheasant could not remain dead in the water while awaiting the dinghy's repeated returns to reload. Instead, she remained outside the reefs where it was too deep to drop anchor, so she steamed back and forth, parallel to the reefs.

Albert Town is situated on the northern coast of Long Cay and in those days, this was the administrative seat, the location of the Commissioner's office for Acklins and Crooked Island. Surely, an event as the arrival of the mail boat, even in the hours before daybreak, would warrant the freight master, Ephraim and other Long Cay residents, to the shore to meet the boat.

Daddy moved with his small tribe from the sandy beach to higher ground, to ready us for our three-mile hike across Long Cay in the pitch dark. Inquisitive me, decided to glance at the sights around us. I was startled to see a huge monster, crouching in the dark behind some trees, ready to pounce on us. With my big strong daddy beside me, my fears soon dissipated, realizing he would protect us. This spooky creature turned out to be nothing but the long government building by the bay that housed the Commissioner's office.

With Sharon on his shoulders and two suitcases in his hands, I followed closely behind Daddy in case another shadowy figure appeared. We were alone on this dark track road that cut across Long Cay from north to south. Mosquitoes pounded us along the way. Sharon complained and scratched her arms and legs as daddy repeatedly tried to comfort her with "We soon reach". I refused to complain.

This path took us through a broad shallow basin, once a salt pan. Unused for many years, the pan became filled with weeds. In the old days, salt pan was flooded with sea water which, when left to evaporate, became rock or coarse salt for sale in Nassau.

When we reached our destination, the little dock on the southern side of Long Cay, we were surprised to meet Uncle Bruce with his brood of two. All we had to do then was wait for "Ole Heif" (Wilfred Hanna) to arrive in his sailboat, the "Silver Lake". Ole Heif was responsible for collecting the mail from Long Cay and take it across the twenty-seven-mile Bight of Acklins to Pompey Bay.

Pompey Bay

A host of noisy, excited relatives was on the Pompey Bay beach to greet us with kisses and hugs. Mama Carrie, our grandmother, the most elated of all, smothered us with affection. This was the first time she was seeing her grandchildren. I don't remember grandpa there to greet us.

A few years ago, I returned to Pompey Bay and my grandparent's house was pointed out to me. I was shocked! I couldn't believe it! This was a fraction of the size I remembered it at the age of seven.

It was a typical Pompey Bay house. Four exterior walls made of lime and stones (rubble). The interior was partitioned into four rooms with wood. There was a front (sitting) room, two bedrooms and a washroom.

The number of windows to a room depended on the number of rubble available to it. Each window had a handmade shutter, which was kept open with a stick during the day. There were two doors to the exterior, one to the front and the other at the washroom in back. The rooms were modestly furnished with the bare essentials. The front room where guests were welcomed, held a rocking chair, two or three sitting chairs, and a tiny table for a kerosene lamp, all skillfully made by hand. Each tiny bedroom held an iron bedstead, clothes closet crudely made and fixed to a corner that hid its contents with a curtain. A galvanized tin tub for bathing was the only thing in the bathroom.

The kitchen was a separate building. In case of fire, the dwelling house would not be in danger. The kitchen was fitted with a stone fire hearth and chimney. The fire hearth always seemed to have live coals even when Mama Carrie was not cooking.

The first thing in the morning, after brushing our teeth, Sharon and I had to go through the ordeal of consuming bay geranium (a type of bush medicine). Mama Carrie stood over us with two cans of this concoction to "clean our blood". I soon realized it was useless to go against Mama Carrie's cool tenacity and gentle persistence. She refused to budge, no matter how much Sharon sobbed, refusing to drink her portion. I threw my can to my head and gulped mine down to get it over with. Man, that bay geranium tasted terrible! It was bitter as gal and Mama Carrie added salt and sour to the brew. Afterward we had breakfast in the kitchen.

Breakfast consisted of bread and the beautiful red colored brazillets tea, (made from a bush), and sweetened with condensed milk. Tall, lanky Grandpa Alvin Tynes did not have much to say to anyone. He sat in the kitchen in his favorite chair, sipping heavily from a large peach can of hot coffee, and a big slice of fresh homemade bread. He would say goodbye and proceed to untie his donkey from a nearby tree. The donkey immediately started jogging on its way and Grandpa would make a mad rush to jump onto the donkey's hind part. It was even more amusing to see Grandpa bounce up and down on this critter's rear with his legs sticking out on both sides, like a bird's out spread wings, while in flight, with his feet shod in wompus.
Despite my frequent pleas, Grandpa never took me to the field with him. He argued it was too far or the road was too rugged for me to

travel. Mama Carrie backed his contention. (I believe she wanted me to be with her.) On Grandpa's return from the field in the afternoon, he would walk behind the donkey, holding the reins. The donkey would be laden with bundles of firewood on its back and sarong baskets full of goodies for his grandchildren over its shoulders. These treats were sugar cane, sweet potatoes, green corn or other goodies, which Mama Carrie prepared for us the next day. She would roast the corn and potatoes on live coals in the hearth and shuck, disjoint and quarter the sugar cane joints for Sharon and me.

By the time Grandpa returned from the field, Sharon and I would already be bathed and Mama Carrie would have completed picking the jiggers from our feet. As she prepared supper, Grandpa seized the opportunity to entertain his grandchildren. Sitting in favorite chair, with his grandchildren on his knees, he told us stories about a character named Bam Bam Suki, none of which I can remember. He would bounce us like galloping horses rhythmically on his knees, rhyming in time with his bouncing knees: "Bam Bam Suki never had a wife, never had a wife till tomorrow night!"

My grandparents kept a hog in a crude pen near the house. The hog ate sumptuously from the kitchen and food from the field. He was well taken care of and I don't remember the hog pen smelling. Mama Carrie warned us constantly not to go near for fear of getting jiggers in our feet. That warning didn't matter because we got jiggers in our feet anyway. In fact, they were in the dust in the yard.

Jiggers in the Bahamian name for chiggers. These flea-like insects bore into the soles of your feet if you walked about the yard barefoot like Sharon and I did. In the afternoon, Mama Carrie would sit with us on the back door steps and commence to pry these critters from the soles of our feet, using a pin. Sharon returned to Nassau with a jigger in her foot. Mommy was so distraught by this, she swore the next time Daddy went to Acklins, he would go alone.

One day while still in Acklins and having no playmates, Mama Carrie sensed boredom. Straightaway she heated some sand in a cast iron pot, dropped three or four hands full of corn in the pot. BINGO! We had popcorn! No salt.

After breakfast, Mama Carrie would prepare lunch to take to school. She would proceed to a fire in the yard where bread was baking in a Dutch oven. This cast iron pot would be sitting on a bed of live coals with another bed of coals on top. To this day, I refer to this as "fire on top and fire on the bottom". Mama Carrie used a stick to move the top bed of coals and turn the Dutch oven over and catch the bread in a towel she held in the other hand. When done, she sliced this bread and made condensed milk sandwiches. These were the rage at school because I hardly ate any of these sandwiches. The children begged me for most of them.

Mama Carrie insisted that Sharon and I wait for Iris and Ruby Tynes to collect us for school. With condensed milk sandwiches in brown paper bags, an exercise book and pencil each, Sharon and I left for school and returned, holding these two big girl's hands. I was barefoot and probably Sharon wore shoes as we walked the sandy beach to the Pompey Bay All-Age School.

The Pompey Bay School is the same building where our ancestors received their primary and secondary education, before they left the island for places around the world. If they returned today, they would recognize this building by its external appearance. It has not changed. Today the school serves as a high school for the island of Acklins.

Imagine both high and primary school classes in the same room, with different subjects taught at the same time. This was when a blackboard was black and supported by an easel. Five to seven students sat on long wooden benches. Our teachers seemed ever so young. DESPITE THESE ADVERSE CONDITIONS, THIS SCHOOL HAS BEEN THE BREEDING GROUND FOR PROFESSIONALS OF MANY KINDS! (PRAISE GOD!!)

One day Sharon and I missed Daddy. He could not be found anywhere. Mama Carrie told us, "He went fishing". Night came and Daddy did not come home before bedtime. Morning and afternoon came and went without Daddy being home. In the afternoon, Mama Carrie called Sharon and me to follow her to the beach, where the other Pompey Bayans were headed. On the horizon was a speck from which came the mournful call of a conch shell horn. This signaled to those at home that the fishermen were returning. This gradually turned out to be a dinghy boat with men in it. When the dinghy was closer to shore, I recognized Daddy amongst the fishermen. When the dinghy was no longer buoyant, the men got out, and with all hands on both sides, lifted the dinghy onto the beach. The boat was turned over to spill its contents of fish on the sand. The Pompey Bayans gathered for their households and went their various ways. But Sharon and I were just happy to have our Daddy back with us.

Cousin Nellie Hanna Major 1933-2013

Nellie Hanna Major was born in Pompey Bay to Clarence and Edith Hanna. She was the granddaughter of Thomas Napoleon and Gram Ella Hanna, great granddaughter of George Hanna, great great granddaughter of John Hanna II. She eventually moved to Nassau and became a nurse. She submits this memory.

Nellie Hanna Major

"Nellie's Childhood Memory on Acklins Island"

When I was a child about seven years old, there lived an elderly lady by the name of Sylvia Tynes. We called her "Aunt Silvie". Now Aunt Silvie had a small grocery shop and my mother, along with other neighbors called this shop of hers a "petty shop". It was a happy time when my mother would ask who wanted to go and purchase a pound or so of sugar. In those days, there was more brown sugar than the now common white sugar. It would take about ten minutes going to and from the shop. After Aunt Silvie weighed the sugar, she would put a lump of brown sugar in the palm of your hand as a treat. One would eat the sugar lump oh so very slowly, so that it would last you the length of the brief walk home. So, we will always remember Aunt Silvie as being kind because of the lump of sweet brown sugar.

Sylvia Heastie Tynes was the daughter of Christopher Heastie and Flora Clark Heastie, granddaughter of Stuart Heastie, and great granddaughter of George Heastie. She was also Edward Heastie's sister. She married Mathias Tynes and had 10 children.

(Elva has fond memories of a favorite aunt who lived next door to her when she was a small child, affectionately called "Aunt Coolie". Aunt Coolie or Virginia Tynes Pratt spent time teaching young Elva how to make small fruit pies and cakes. Her house was a fascinating place with ducks, chickens, tropical fruits and plants all around. Every day after school, young Elva looked forward to dropping by her house to see what goodies were in store for her. Virginia Tynes Pratt was the daughter of Aunt Silvie, mentioned above.)

Aunt Sylvia Heastie Tynes and a relative

Aunt Coolie (VirginiaTynes Pratt), Sylvias daughter

Elva's Memory of Aunt Coolie: The first house I remember living in was located on 64th street between 18 and 19th avenue in Liberty City, Miami (1926-1934). Aunt Coolie lived next door. I called her aunt, but she was really my cousin, my father's sister Sylvia's child. I loved visiting her and she had a great influence on me. Although I was under the age of 8, but she would teach me how to bake little pies and cakes. She had a duck pond in her yard and raised baby ducks, chickens and rabbits. There were all kinds of fruit trees and interesting flowers growing in her yard. Aunt Coolie always had time for me and I loved playing there.

Cousin Ruby Tynes Ferguson

Ruby Ferguson, a direct descendant of Dr. Benjamin Tynes, shares some of her memories growing up on Acklins Island. She is a descendant through her father Clayton Tynes, whose father was Theophilus Tynes, whose father was Charles Tynes, whose father was Dr. William James Tynes, whose father was Dr. Bejamin Tynes. She was born in 1936 and grew up on Acklins until she married and moved to Nassau at 19. Her mother had two older sons, but several miscarriages before Ruby was born, so her mother went to Nassau to have baby Ruby in a hospital, before returning to Acklins. Ruby grew up in the Tynes yard and has many fond memories.

"Cousin Ruby's Memories"

I remember life on Acklins as a very happy time. My playmates were all cousins who lived the Tynes or Hanna Big Yard. Some of my playmates were Iris, Mavis, Lydia, Amanda and Beverly Tynes. We had parties and dances on some weekends and special occasions. Family members would play instruments and dance to the music. Although there was no electricity or TV sets, my family did have a wind up victrola, which could play music. We entertained each other with the resources we had. As children, we swam in the ocean and played with dolls and marbles.

The families were very close and supported each other. I remember some of the relatives who lived in the Tynes and Hanna yards. Each had their own houses. Hilton Tynes, Jarvis Tynes, my grandfather, Theophilus Tynes, Alvin Tynes, Curtis Tynes, Stanley Tynes, Roland Tynes, Henry Tynes, William Tynes, Linda Tynes and her parents, Clayton Tynes and Harriet Hanna, Aunt Kitty Tynes, Mathias Tynes were a few in the Tynes yard. Clarence Hanna, Gram Ella, Wilfred Hanna, Oscar Hanna, Rufus Hanna, and George Hanna were a few in the Hanna yard. We were all family.

The men built their own houses. They were brick with shingle roofs. Most had 3 rooms with a separate kitchen unattached. Most people had no glass windows, but windows made of wooden shutters. It would be very dark inside if the windows were closed. But we had kerosene lamps and lanterns for light. The mosquitoes and sand flies were horrible, but a fire lit outside would keep mosquitoes away. Mosquitoes were particularly bad after a rainy day.

We all attended the same school and church. The school was called the Pompey Bay All Age School and was a one room schoolhouse. All the children were taught in one room, from grades 1-6. One of my teachers was Hester Tynes, a relative. The church, St. Aidens Anglican Church, was a huge building. It was right between the Hanna Big Yard and the Tynes yard. The church was the center of our lives. Church service was 11:00 each Sunday, with Sunday school at 3 or 4pm and another service at 7 pm. Most relatives were baptized, confirmed, married and funeralized there. Most of the members were from the Hanna and Tynes families. The priest was stationed at Long Cay and would come for special occasions. The catechist conducted the service each Sunday. Most catechists were family members. My Uncle Curtis Tynes was a catechist one time, while I was growing up there.

Most families had small boats for fishing and travel. The men built the boats. There were no cars on the island at that time, however some had bikes. We walked everywhere, unless we traveled to another island. We took sail boats to Nassau and other islands. Sometimes it would take many weeks, if the weather was bad. Some got very sea sick and there were no life vests, like they have today. The women and men slept in separate cabins under the deck of the boat. There was no bathroom facility. Wastes were brought up on deck and dumped overboard from buckets. Sometimes animals were also being transported. They were kept in a pen on one side of the deck of the boat. The top deck had a place to cook food for the passengers. There might be about 20 passengers on the boat sailing to other islands. We would sing songs and tell stories to keep entertained. If the weather was good, you could get to Nassau in 3 or 4 days., but we were dependent on the wind. The mail came by boat about every 2 weeks. Everyone would look forward to mail day and would gather at the dock waiting to see if they got any.

Eric Wiberg writes about the Hanna family's experience with shipping in his book, "Mailboats of the Bahamas, Two Hundred Years of Maritime History."
"From the early 1800 to 1911 members of the Hanna family owned ten vessels of various sizes in the Bahamas. In 1868, William H. Hanna of Long Bay, Crooked Island owned a 19-ton schooner named Augusta Justina. In 1935, Castell Rivas Hanna of Pompey Bay owned the sloop, Delightful. By 1911

five other Hannas from Acklins owned the locally built schooners; Barbara Ellen, Charm, Excite, Mary and Sea Bird. Their owners were John James, Phillip Hannah, Conrad C., William H. and Thomas Benjamin Hanna. J.E. Hanna owned the schooner, Molly, registered to Grand Bahama. Alexander Hanna owned the 9-ton schooner, Venus, in Crooked Island. So, 100 years ago, the family was already a vessel-owning dynasty, however modest some of the craft may have been."

My father, Clayton Tynes, was a carpenter by trade and mother was a seamstress. All the women made clothes for their families with fabric purchased in Nassau or other places. The men fished and cleaned the fish on the beach. All that was not eaten that day was salted to preserve it, as there was no refrigeration. There was a salt pond on the island and salt accumulated along the edge of the pond. You could just go and scoop up what you needed. We used canned milk most of the time. Conch was dried on a string and was a popular dish served. But we also ate other types of meats like chickens, and hogs that were raised on the island. Although Acklins is rocky, there are areas where farming was done and they grew lots of fruits and veggies. We always had plenty to eat. Most families had their own well for fresh water. The wells were dug inland and the deeper you dug, the more fresh water you had. A paint can was used to retrieve the water. There were no pumps.

I remember the time my grandfather, Theophilus Tynes, died. When a person died, there would be a 'wake" where the body would be brought to the family home and set up in the living room. Family members would visit and stay up all night, singing, mourning, and having coffee and bread. The next day the body would be brought to St. Aiden's church for a funeral and then buried immediately after the funeral. I remember helping my uncle tote the heavy tomb that was placed on my grandfather's grave. Not all graves had headstones. Family members were buried in a family grave a little way off from the Big Yard. But one family member was buried in the church yard. That was

William Alexander "Backay" Hanna, because he was a catechist.

I have many memories of growing up on my island home, Acklins. It was a happy time of love and family.

Clayton Tynes, Ruby's father

Cousin Hazel Helen Heastie Meade

Hazel Helen Heastie Meade is the daughter of Arthur Arnold Heastie (March 1, 1910 - 1944) and granddaughter of William Heastie. She was born August 24, 1936, in Belle Glade, Florida. Her family moved to Miami, Florida while she was still an infant. Later she moved to New York City, where she married Richard Meade. They have two daughters, Mary Elaine Meade-Montague and Karen Ann Meade-Wilson. In her career, she served in roles of teacher, principal and adjunct professor in New York City schools and colleges. She's an ordained Elder at the Brooklyn Seventh-day Adventist Church and currently resides in Massachusetts.

Helen Heastie Meade and husband, Richard

William Henry Heastie and children, Arthur, James and May

"Memories of Uncle Willie"
by Hazel H. Meade

Uncle Willie (William Heastie), my grandfather, was one of the sons of Christopher Heastie, who was son of Stuart Heastie, who was the son of the original George Heastie. He was one of many relatives who migrated to the United States, by way of Miami, Florida. One of his brothers, Edward Heastie, also migrated to Florida. Many immigrants settled in Florida because of the opportunities for work. Some worked on the Biscayne Causeway which linked Miami with Miami Beach. The rich black soil of the Everglades gave promise of great prospects for enterprise. Some migrants farmed the land and picked fruit. But William, an entrepreneur, chose to go to the Everglades and Belle Glade area to provide services to migrant workers. He operated a store, a restaurant and boarding house in Belle Glade in the early 1930s.

Edward, his brother, chose to live in Miami and commute to the fields to work.

William Henry, warmly known as Uncle Willie, has been described as a tall man who wore overalls and a straw hat. This was his daily attire, but on Sundays he dressed formally in a suit, tie and fashionable hat. He sometimes drove a truck to distribute farm goods and sometimes drove a Model T Ford. We know that he loved his children and doted on his grandchildren. In the few pictures we have of him, he is pictured with his children and granddaughter, Rachel. William also encouraged his children educationally and never tried to interrupt them when they were reading.

Ruth, May's oldest daughter. Was Uncle Willies first grandchild. She remembers riding in the back seat of his brand-new Model T Ford. She remembers speaking to him in a stuttering voice, trying to express herself, which was a speech impediment she had. He looked back at her form the driver's seat and said, "Stop all that stuttering!" Ruth said that from then on, she was cured of stuttering.

Elva remembers that her father Edward, (Uncle Willies brother), would travel from Miami to work in the fields of Belle Glade, Florida. While there, he stayed with Uncle Willie. Uncle Willie even built a small house for his brother so that he could live comfortably whenever he came up there to work. One fateful stormy day, while in Belle Glade, Uncle Eddie went under a tree to wait for the rain to stop. He lit his pipe and was fatally stuck by lightning.

Uncle Willie had a reputation for being kind and generous. After Uncle Eddies death, Uncle Willie continued to look out for Eddies wife (Katie) and children by bringing fresh produce and money whenever he came to Miami. Uncle Willie would take Grace, Elva's youngest sister, for long visits, to help out. Grace remembers Uncle Willie teaching her to write. She also remembers sitting next to him at a big table in his boarding house where he carefully watched over her. One of the highlights of her visit was going on a plane ride with him. It was a rare occasion, because there were few planes around in those days and it was obviously a joyride. She remembers sitting on his lap and holding tightly to him.

Willies' son, Arthur Arnold and his wife Hazel lived with him. Hazel said that her father-in-law was well respected in the community. He had dealings with both white and black. Once he had a disagreement with a white man and cursed at him saying, "By God!". Swearing in God's name was not taken lightly in those days. Considering the times, it was not acceptable for a black man, no matter how affluent they were, to swear at a white man. The man took Uncle Willie to court and the judge did not take this case lightly. But Uncle Willie said, "Sure I said it because by God we live and by God we die!" The judge didn't buy his answer. He probably had to pay a fine or endure a strong admonition.

During the time that Artur and Hazel lived with Uncle Willie, their first daughter, Shirley, was born in 1934. Hazel said that Uncle Willie took Shirley everywhere with him, like it was his child.

One Sunday afternoon, Uncle Willie ate lunch and went to take a bath in preparation for attending a funeral. He died suddenly while in the bath tub, of a heart attack.

We are privileged to be a part of our Hanna, Heastie, Tynes heritage. All that we are and hope to be had been built on a firm foundation of our forefathers with the grace of our Lord and savior Jesus Christ. May God continue to bless us with His Spirit as we continue to carry on and be faithful to our prosperity.

William Heastie and granddaughter, Rachel Rolle

Elva's Memories
"Working in Miami 1946-47"

Many family members from Acklins Island migrated over the years. They migrated to Nassau and other Bahamian islands, the United States, as well as other countries. The main reason was to find better paying jobs. My parents moved to Miami, Florida for just that reason. Although they always planned to return to the Bahamas to live, it never happened. I was born and raised in Miami Florida, but went to college/nursing school in the north.

Mercy-Douglass Hospital School of Nursing was an African American hospital and the first school for black nurses in Philadelphia, Pa. It operated from 1895-1960. In August of 1946, I was thrilled to have completed three years of nursing school. WWII had just ended and the boys were returning home from overseas. Life for me then, could not have been brighter.

Returning home to Miami, I looked to my oldest sister, Idella, for directions. She usually made all the family decisions since my father s death in 1934, and this was no exception. Idella was 11 years older than me and also a registered nurse. I joined the staff at Jackson Memorial Hospital (J.M.H.) where Idella was already employed.

Idella and Elva Heastie

The only other hospital in the city for black nurses to seek employment was a small private one (Christian Hospital), born out of segregation. Here was a place black doctors could take their patients. They were usually middle-class black patients who did not want to be in the open "charity wards" at J.M.H., nor did they wish to be treated by white physicians. For the most part, many felt white physicians could not be trusted to care for them with integrity and a caring manner. This was not without foundation.

Nearly all of the black nurses (about 20 in all) at J.M.H. had been there for years. Idella was among the youngest and more knowledgeable of recent trends in nursing. She seemed to be held in high esteem.

Shortly before my arrival, the hospital added a new wing to its building. They moved what appeared to be their charity ward for white patients into this new area and moved the black patients into this newly vacated area, formerly used by the white patients. This however was a vast improvement over the old "Colored Ward" from the past. Black people were very happy about his, including myself.

Now we had one whole floor for medical patients and one whole floor for surgical patients. There were a few rooms with 4 or 6 beds, when before, we had one long room for men and one long room for women, regardless of the diagnosis. The only privacy was a curtain between the beds. Overflow children were thrown in with the women, as the pediatric room was very small. Tubercular patients were at the end of this room for a time, so you can see this move to a new area was a cause for rejoicing.

There were no black doctors on staff at this time. Black nurses took care of only black patients. There was no mixing of the races except as for the white doctors/black patients, and white supervisors.

White nurses were addressed as "Miss", while black nurses were addressed as "Nurse". But since I had been trained in the north (Philadelphia, PA), I found this rule demeaning and said so. The use of "Miss Heastie", as I answered the phone etc., made the black nurses feel uncomfortable and somehow, I did not fit in. Idella was not able to persuade me that it didn't matter, and this annoyed the white people, nurses and otherwise.

The nursing office called me in about this, but I refused to give in. Near the end of my first year, one supervisor decided she had enough of my "insubordination", confronted me in the hallway, insisting that I follow protocol immediately. I asked her why she felt that I owed her more respect than I was willing to give myself? In fact, my exact words were, "What makes you think I think more of you than I do myself?" "Because it's the law!", was her answer. The next day I gave my 30-day notice and left J.M.H. never to return as a nurse there. Years later, after many changes, and we were treated differently, I gave birth to my daughter there.

Before leaving J.M.H., I heard the Veterans Administration opened a hospital using one of the hotels on Miami Beach, to care for returning veterans from WWII. As a result of the U.S. government financing the later 2/3 of my nursing education (The Cadet Nurse Corp), I applied for a job there. If they hired me, this would have been breaking new ground for black nurses and I would be thrilled!

I remember making a flawless appearance in uniform. My manners were impeccable and I knew my performance as a nurse was excellent. At the interview my credentials were reviewed sympathetically. I was told, "We really would like to hire you, but we can only hire white nurses. We are so sorry." Somehow, I believed this nurse was sincere. I thanked her, went home and applied to the University of Chicago Lying-In Hospital in Illinois. I was accepted immediately and started working there in October of 1947. Idella had mixed emotions. My mother was tearful.

Some time after this, Idella told me this practice had been dropped and all nurses were called the same, Miss or Mrs., as the case may be. To some this might seem like a small thing, but it digs deep into the hearts and minds of a people to conform to second citizenship. I don't know when things changed for the black physician, but I do know that this attitude still exists today in the hearts and minds of some white people. Black people are able to see this clearly, like an iridescent light in the dark, and many react to it, not always politely.

Elva Heastie Gamble as a young student nurse, 1947

Katie Heastie said that on Acklins there was no animosity between the races. There were only a few whites on the island like the bishop or the commissioner, so there was no need to suppress black people there. Although they were poor, they were free and treated equally and did not have the experiences of blacks in the U.S.

Words of Wisdom to My Grandchildren by Elva Heastie Gamble

"My wish for my grandchildren is that they begin each day with a grateful heart and that they exhibit integrity at every turn. Begin each day by asking God, "What would you have me to do today?" It has been said that we make our plans and God makes His plans. In time we learn our plans don't matter very much. This is the best route to a satisfying life, which I pray for each of them, each day."

Tribute to Honorable AD Hanna and Carl Heastie Jr

The Hanna, Heastie Tynes families have produced great leaders in the US, Bahamas and abroad. Family members have excelled in many areas. Two notable examples are Arthur Dion Hanna and Carl Heastie Jr.

Honorable Arthur Dion Hanna: A.D. Hanna was born in 1928 on Pompey Bay, Acklins Island and died in 2021. A.D. Hanna served as the 8th Governor General of the Bahamas. He attended the Pompey Bay All Age school at an early age, before finishing his education in Nassau and London, where he received his law degree from the British Bar. He was also Deputy Prime Minister from 1967-1984. He played an instrumental role in helping the Bahamas obtain independence. In 2014, the first Legend- class patrol boat of the Royal Bahamas Defense Force was commissioned as "HMBS Arthur Dion Hanna". His latest honor was having his photo printed on the Bahamian $100.00 bill. He was the son of Joseph Albert Hanna, the grandson of Estell Hanna Heastie and great grandson of Conrad Crosby Hanna and a direct descendant of John Hanna.

Speaker Carl Heastie Jr.: Born in 1967 in New York City, Carl is a descendant of John Hanna by way of his grandmother, Katie Hanna Heastie and a descendant of George Heastie, by way of his grandfather, Edward Heastie. He has served in the New York State Assembly and was elected Speaker of the Assembly in 2015. He was the first African American to be elected in this position. Through his leadership, he has influenced legislation that has impacted the lives of many in positive ways and is an example of the success and progress of the Hanna, Heastie Tynes family.

Honorable Carl Heastie and his daughter, Taylor

Conclusion by Judith Bell

I remember my grandmother, Katie Hanna Heastie. She was short, stout and fair skinned with long wavy hair that she wrapped in a twist behind her head. She was slew footed and talked with a thick Bahamian accent. She made fudge for us and taught her granddaughters to crochet. She had high expectations for us (morally) and gave plenty of love. But what I remember most was her strong belief in God and her commitment to family. Those are values she learned from our ancestors who lived on Acklins Island, Bahamas so many years ago. It is my hope that through this book, these stories of our family members will be preserved, other family members will be inspired to record stories, and generations to come will learn about our history. It is through remembering our past that we will come to know ourselves and continue to pass down those values that we hold so dear, to future generations.

For more information visit the family website: hannaian.com/family (this website may be under review)

Judith Bell and Samuel Hanna

www.ingramcontent.com/pod-product-compliance
Lightning Source LLC
Chambersburg PA
CBHW031653040426
42453CB00006B/295